LifeCaps Presents:

The Real Life Mary Poppins
The Life and Times of P.L. Travers

By Paul Brody

BookCaps™ Study Guides
www.bookcaps.com

© 2013. All Rights Reserved.

Cover Image © greiss design - Fotolia.com

Table of Contents

About LifeCaps

LifeCaps is an imprint of BookCaps™ Study Guides. With each book, a lesser known or sometimes forgotten life is is recapped. We publish a wide array of topics (from baseball and music to literature and philosophy), so check our growing catalogue regularly (**www.bookcaps.com**) to see our newest books.

Introduction

Among twentieth century authors, P. L. Travers was by far the most productive and famous to hail from the British colony of Australia. After a brief and modestly successful acting career, she moved to London and pursued her own brand of journalism. She was a well-regarded drama critic and travel author, and she became friends with many influential writers and thinkers on both sides of the Atlantic Ocean. Eventually, she found her greatest voice in the form of Mary Poppins, the mysterious and powerful Edwardian nanny. Thirty years after the first Poppins adventure is published, Walt Disney produced a live-action movie version, which has ingrained itself forever in the popular imagination.

Chapter One: The Early Life of P. L. Travers (Helen Lyndon Goff)

P. L. Travers was born Helen Lyndon Goff in Queensland, Australia in August 1899. The eldest of three children, Goff's parents, Margaret Morehead and Travers Robert Goff, were originally from England. Robert had made his way to Australia in search of a stable career, while Margaret came from a relatively rich family of businessmen and traders. Growing up in a home infused with traditions of the "Mother Country" in the exotic setting of the Australian countryside no doubt had profound effects on all the Goff children.

Robert died unexpectedly when Goff was only seven, leaving her with only fanciful, childlike memories of a man who dreamed of a mythical homeland. The memory of her father would become a powerful influence on Goff's work throughout her life. She recalled her father as a well-to-do planter on a sugarcane plantation, but this was far from the real story. In fact, Robert Goff was a former bank manager at the Australian Joint Stock Bank who had been demoted to the lowly position of bank clerk. At that point, the family patriarch was barely capable of making ends meet and supporting the family. To make matters worse, he had a weakness for alcohol, and by most accounts, his life never measured up to his dreams and grand ideas.

Like so many with alcohol problems, Robert Goff had a romantic but impractical outlook on life. He had a deep love and admiration for the myths and literature of his adopted homeland, Ireland. Though born in London, he typically presented himself to the world as an Irishman at heart. He had a fascination with elves, fairies and magic. When drinking, Robert typically entertained (or bored) guests with well-known Irish poetry and folk tales. Again, this curious turn of mind likely had a formative role in the imagination of the young Helen Lyndon Goff. She even took his Christian name – Travers – as her surname when she created her pen name.

From her mother came Goff's sense of aristocracy and privilege. Margaret Morehead was the granddaughter of the shrewd, wealthy businessman Robert Archibald Alison Morehead. He made his fortune in property and commodities, always careful with his investments. The senior Morehead also worked hard to ensure that his offspring would be well provided for. He and his wife Helen had four children of their own, two boys and two girls. Margaret's father, Robert Charles, succumbed to tuberculosis at the age of 32, an event that would later fill Goff's impressionable imagination with an intense dread of disease in general, and TB specifically.

A rift between Margaret's mother, Maria, and her grandfather, Robert, led to tense relations and the rewriting of wills. Eventually, Margaret was taken into custody by an unmarried aunt while her mother remarried – the remarriage being the main point of conflict within the Morehead family. Margaret's aunt – Helen, or "Aunt Ellie" – would eventually become one of the inspirations for the Mary Poppins character. Helen's brother Boyd, on the other hand, became a cautionary tale of excessive ambition and poor management of money. Boyd more or less single-handedly squandered Margaret's share of her grandfather's estate. In the nineteenth century, a woman with little capital of her own had severely limited prospects. Her slim income may have been a deciding factor in accepting the marriage proposal of Travers Robert Goff, who was preparing to take his bank position in Sydney. At the time, he seemed a picture of reliability, with a cosmopolitan air and good sense of humor. He was a convenient match, but perhaps not the match she would have made had her financial outlook been less uncertain.

Margaret and Robert's first child, Helen Lyndon Goff, was born in 1899. By then, the family had relocated to Maryborough, an agricultural hamlet on the Australian east coast, about 160 miles north of Brisbane. As a child, Goff was known simply as "Lindy" or "Ginty." She is only a baby when she first encounters Aunt Ellie, the powerful figure who was in many ways the real parental force in Margaret's life. Unbeknownst to them at the time, Aunt Ellie would again be thrust into the role of second mother when circumstances turned sour for the Goffs.

In contrast with her father's heavy drinking and continual disappointments, Aunt Ellie represented a stabilizing force. In a sense, young Goff was the product of three adult influences rather than two. The mannerisms, habits, sayings and values of Aunt Ellie were a strong force during Goff's childhood and early adolescence. When the family suffered trials and tribulations, she was a sanctuary against the storm. Her clever and instructional sayings became part of Goff's own approach to the problems of life. Later, these bits of real-life detail would find creative expression in the character of Mary Poppins.

Aunt Ellie's house in Sydney became a sort of home away from home for Margaret and the baby, with Robert writing romantic letters to his wife from Maryborough. At other times, Margaret would go on a trip, and the children would be left to Robert and a nanny. Goff's parents were somewhat detached, which was typical for the period, and they were happy to leave their children to their own devices. Likewise, neither Margaret nor Robert Goff were quick to answer any of life's momentous, difficult questions. Goff, therefore, developed a brooding, meditative frame of mind from an early age. Later in life, this brooding evolved into a fierce kind of independence and even reclusiveness. As a youth, she had a fascination with hens and chickens, in particular the way in which they sat for days on end keeping their eggs warm, "brooding."

In 1902, the Goff family left Maryborough for Brisbane. Robert had most likely been demoted from his position as bank manager. As an ordinary bank clerk, he frequently had to travel far and wide filling in for other bank employees. In the Goff household, two new children arrived - Barbara Ierne in 1902 and Cicely Margaret in 1905. However, any chance for domestic bliss was replaced by uncertainty, money problems and Robert's increased drinking.

Robert was once again transferred, this time to the small town of Allora, many miles inland from Brisbane. It was in Allora that Goff learned all of the southern constellations. The night sky fired her imagination, but she felt a strange foreboding during twilight. At the same time, she became a voracious reader. Her favorites were the Bible and Grimms' fairy tales, mostly for the same reason. Goff had an attraction to "dark" characters, evil stepmothers, witches, etc. In the Australian outback, light and dark, fantasy and reality all felt like shades of the same color.

Robert Goff fell gravely ill in 1907. He struggled for a few days, and then quickly succumbed to a fever. Though only a child, Goff realized that his heavy drinking likely contributed to his death. The family is left penniless, but not entirely hopeless. The charity of relatives – Aunt Ellie in particular – enables life to go on for the Goff family with something approaching normalcy. On the urging of Aunt Ellie, the family relocates to a cottage in Bowral, a quaint town outside of Sydney and away from the sweltering summer heat of the coast.

In Bowral, Helen Lyndon Goff grows from a child into a young woman. Those closest to her realize that she has a keen intellect and a mischievous personality. She makes many friends, some of whom will one day provide fodder for her writing career. In 1912, Aunt Ellie secures a place for inquisitive young niece at Normanhurst Private Girls School in Sydney. She's resentful at first at having to leave the quiet and comfort of Bowral, but she quickly adapts to life among her peers.

Normanhurst is a revelation for Goff. She is introduced to new art forms and new modes of thinking that will leave a lasting impact on the budding writer. At first, her behavior is less than ideal, but she quickly adapts. It helps that her instructors, including the principal Beatrice Tildsley, can see the intelligent, charming young woman underneath of her antics and outbursts. She explains to her instructors that books are her favorite things, and she is often given the liberty to sit in the library and read to her heart's content. The atmosphere of the school is so vastly different from Bowral that it's like an awakening for Goff. Were it not for the charity and insight of Aunt Ellie, she might have lived out her life, unknown and unremarkable, in the backcountry of Australia.

Chapter Two: Acting and Early Career

Before she became a respected drama critic and later world famous as the author of the Mary Poppins series of books, Helen Lyndon Goff tested the waters of an acting career. At Normanhurst Private Girls School, she had her first, transformative experience with theater. She takes a music class for fun, through which she discovers the joys of theater. Upon witnessing a school play in which the hero is drenched in fake blood, she has a life-altering epiphany: She realizes that her life's wish is to be part of the spectacle of theater, not merely an observer. Goff begins writing about theater for the school paper, and she attends every locally produced theatrical performance that she possibly can. In school, her instructors recognize both her grasp of language (which will help her as a journalist) and keen eye for the nuances of the stage.

In November 1914, Goff produced a fundraising variety show and concert for the war effort. The First World War, then known as The Great War, had just commenced, and Australia, as a territory of the United Kingdom, was deeply committed to the conflict. Goff's production included both comedy and drama. The most memorable part was an intensely dramatic scene of kings, knights and beautiful ladies in distress. The show concluded with the "death" of Kaiser Wilhelm and English victory in the war. The fundraiser was a smashing success, and only added more fuel to Goff's fiery ambition.

Her instructors weren't the only ones to notice the extraordinary talent and creativity of the young Goff girl from Bowral. The London-born drama and speech coach Lawrence Campbell recognized a future star in the young Australian girl and offered to make her his protégé. At one point, he even suggested that Goff come to live with him and his wife, a somewhat scandalous offer. For reasons of practicality, she declined his offer of hospitality. For one thing, her immediate family looked down their noses at actors. Aunt Ellie would have been horrified had her young niece joined an acting troupe rather than complete her studies. More importantly, Goff understood enough of the world to see the foolishness of moving in with an older man. Still, she took advantage of every opportunity to participate in the theater, no matter how small. She learned all she could from Campbell, and owed much of her theatrical success to his guidance.

In 1915, Campbell cast Goff as "Bottom" in his production of *A Midsummer Night's Dream*, which was performed for a large audience at Sydney's Ashfield Town Hall. She later starred as the title character in *Le Voyage de Monsieur Perrichon*. Goff excelled in her studies at the same time she was earning high praise for her acting work. She easily passed the University Examination. She was awarded the designation of prefect, which granted her some amount of authority over her fellow pupils. Campbell continued to be a guiding, fatherly influence on Goff's development as an artist. He took her, along with several of the older girls from her class, to see a production of *Richard III* at the New Adelphi Theater. The English actor Allan Wilkie played the part of Malvolio with gusto, and the Normanhurst girls were certainly impressed. Wilkie most likely made the biggest impression on Goff, who realized at that moment that the famous actor would make an excellent mentor. It would be years, however, before the two would meet.

Despite these victories, life for the Goff family was not without hardships. When forced to choose between a career of her own and working to support her family, Goff had little choice but to leave acting and writing behind (for a time) and pursue work for the sake of her mother and sisters. She even turned down a scholarship to study in England, because the family was so in need of her assistance. Margaret never quite recovered her balance after the death of Robert, and the eldest daughter was naturally forced to grow up fast.

Aunt Ellie, domineering and practical as always, was the impetus behind Goff getting a job. She walked with her niece to the Australia Gas Light Company, where she had a friend in management. Goff was hired as a typist, which she discovered to be a tedious kind of work, but that fortunately left her mind to wander. Her family desperately needed the money. Aunt Ellie was generous in the sense of empowering others to help themselves. Margaret, Biddy and Moya had recently moved back to Sydney, renting a small house on Pembroke Street in the neighborhood of Ashfield. There was simply no opportunity for a stable life in the resort town of Bowral. Despite her family responsibilities, Goff still dreamed of a life on the stage, hearing the applause of adoring fans.

Even though she spends her day typing letters and forms at the gas light company, Goff still makes time for the finer things in life. She discovers the art of dancing and proves to be a quick study. She takes night classes with Minnie Everett's dance hall in Sydney. Many of the older girls in Everett's class regularly take part in local theatrical productions, as either ballet dancers or members of the chorus. A few even earn small speaking parts. Goff is envious of their opportunities, but her mother and Aunt Ellie continue to resist the idea of pursuing drama as a bona fide career.

In 1920, Goff earned a spot as a pantomime dancer for the production of *Sleeping Beauty*. Aunt Ellie and Margaret pushed back against the idea, but they finally relented and let her take the part. The play ran for six weeks at the Criterion in Sydney. While preparing for her part backstage, Goff met and befriended the famous Irish actress Peggy Doran. She got up the courage to ask if the actress wouldn't mind critiquing her reading of a few lines from *L'Aiglon*. Miss Doran was impressed, and she spread the news around the troupe that the young Goff girl was a real actress in the disguise of a pantomime. Minnie Everett was equally impressed by this news, and insisted that Goff take a speaking role in *Sleeping Beauty*. Apart from her minor performances as a girl at Normanhurst, this was her coming-out party.

After hearing the applause of the audience gathered at the Criterion, there was no going back for Goff. She had found her calling, but she was in need of guidance and instruction – her talents were still raw and incomplete. Campbell had begun the process of crafting her into an actress.
She needed more time and more instruction to realize her gifts.

In 1921, Allan Wilkie would take his place as Goff's new mentor and father figure. Several years earlier, Wilkie and his wife had fled South Africa because of the First World War. With financial support from fellow Englishman George Marlow, Wilkie formed a touring Shakespeare company: Marlow's Grand Shakespeare Company. January 1916 marked the company's debut performance: *The Merchant of Venice*. His new company toured the major cities of Australia, earning high praise from drama critics. At heart, Wilkie was a traditionalist. He frowned upon the modern re-imaginings of Shakespeare that had become so fashionable. Whenever Marlow's Grand Shakespeare Company spent a season in Sydney, Goff was a frequent member of the audience, along with Lawrence Campbell and some of the other Normanhurst girls.

Wilkie parted ways with George Marlow in 1920, choosing to put together a company under his own management. Wilkie's company was slated to perform for six weeks at Sydney's Grand Opera House in February 1921. Prior to the beginning of this season, Goff and Wilkie met in person for the first time, possibly introduced by Lawrence Campbell. Wilkie agreed, reluctantly, to let the spindly young woman audition for the company. Goff was terrified, afraid that she would fail miserably, and her hopes of a show business career be dashed against the rocks.

Goff's audition for Wilkie's company was comical, but it landed her a position. Wilkie asked her to run around a pile of chairs as if she were running around a fountain and being chased by a young man. When a flesh and blood young man captured her and planted a kiss directly on her lips, she slapped him hard. The actor was stunned, and told Wilkie not to hire her. However, Wilkie liked what he saw, and Goff joined the company with a salary of two pounds per week.

The lead actress in all of Allen Wilkie's productions was his wife, Frediswyde Hunter-Watts. Goff began her career as a simple understudy, not expecting to earn serious stage time. If one of the main players became ill, she might be asked to step in for a night or two. Other than that, she was merely there to observe, learn and help the stagehands when necessary. Her mother and Aunt Ellie were supportive of Goff's work this time. They understood that Shakespeare was a notch above ordinary theater, and they knew that Wilkie had a reputation for artistic productions of the highest order. They were still cautious, but now they were cautiously optimistic that their young woman might actually succeed in her unconventional career choice.

Eventually, after much sitting and watching from backstage, Goff got the part of Anne Page in *The Merry Wives of Windsor*. At the debut in March 1921, she was terrified and had a hard time uttering her lines. She could barely bring her voice above the level of a whisper. In the meantime, Wilkie's company was preparing for a trip through all the major cities and towns of Australia and New Zealand. It would be a fantastic chance for Goff to earn wider exposure, as well as learn something more about her corner of the world. Aunt Ellie, however, did not approve of her niece caravanning with a troupe of actors. She strictly forbids the journey, saying she was still too young for such an adventure. Goff was heartbroken, but determined to see her dreams through to the end.

Just as her career was getting its sea legs, Goff began to think that the name "Lyndon Goff" was not particularly attractive, and certainly not theatrical. Most actors chose stage names that had a lyrical quality. She decided that her father's given name, Travers, had a lovely ring to it. Looking at her family tree, she was also intrigued by the name Pamela. The name was coming back into fashion, and Goff thought that "Pamela Travers" sounded like an actress's name much more so than "Lyndon Goff." After about 1921, she rarely if ever referred to herself by her actual birth name.

While Allen Wilkie's company was touring greater Australia and New Zealand, newly christened "Pamela Travers" joined up with a small-time acting troupe in New South Wales. There were only eight players all together, and they traveled from town to town, packed like sardines inside a truck. They staged performances at roadside stands, town fairs, and other temporary, low-budget establishments. The experience was a transformation for Travers and her first taste of real independence. The troupe never played any large concert halls or theaters, but the camaraderie and freedom were unforgettable. Nevertheless, Wilkie had not forgotten about his young understudy. When Wilkie's company returned to Melbourne to prepare for a performance of *Julius Caesar*, he requested that Travers rejoin them as soon as possible.

Travers's second stint as a member of Wilkie's Shakespeare company was even more rewarding than her first. She climbed the ladder from bit parts to leading ladies, including Juliet in *Romeo and Juliet*. Because Wilkie had achieved a certain amount of fame, critics' reviews of his company's performances appeared in the major newspapers. Travers clipped these stories out and mailed them to Aunt Ellie and her mother. She no doubt felt vindicated in her choice of careers. Little did she know at the time that she would soon find herself in another part of the world, following a different path entirely.

Chapter Three: Early Writing Career

While Travers was busy touring with Allan Wilkie's Shakespeare company, she still found time to occasionally compose some occasional verse or the odd essay. Despite her love of performance and exhibition, the writing bug never left her. In March 1922, she published a short, sentimental bit of poetry in *The Triad*, a somewhat lowbrow literary magazine. It's unknown how her first efforts were received by readers. The editors of *The Triad* advertised adult erotic literature in the margins, so the readers were probably mostly male. Her byline for the piece was "Pamela Young Travers," the first and last time she used that particular name. Publication inspired something inside of her, and she began to shift her mental energy away from theater and towards the written word. She was merely waiting for some sign or transforming event to indicate that path she should follow.

It was in 1923 while the company was performing in Christchurch, New Zealand, that circumstances came together to ignite Travers's passion for writing and zest for life. A local journalist for the Christchurch *Sun* saw the young actress in the street one night, partying with her comrades, and became completely smitten. He reportedly began following the company around New Zealand, all for the sake of being close to Travers. She returned his advances, and the pair had a passionate, though brief relationship. Sadly, brief and passionate are fair descriptions of most of her intimate, adult relationships. History does not record the name of this New Zealand lover because of Travers's commitment to keeping her personal details out of print.

The New Zealand journalist encourages Travers to continue writing after she shows him some of her work. He even passes some of the work on to his editor, who is quite impressed. The relationship results in her regular publication in the Christchurch *Sun*. According to Travers, the editor of the paper gladly publishes virtually everything she submits. She gets a thrill seeing her name on the byline, perhaps even more of a thrill than she felt while performing on stage. When the Shakespeare company returns to Australia, Travers continues sending work to the *Sun*. She even gets her own column, "Pamela Passes: The *Sun's* Sydney Letter." The subject matter varied from one issue to the next, but always displayed her unique sense of humor and talent for capturing the fine details of a scene.

Back in Australia, Travers decides to pursue a writing career to the utmost. She begins regularly sending work to literary magazines and periodicals, including the *Shakespearean Quaterly*, *Vision*, and *The Green Room*. She experiments with numerous forms and styles, from poetry to satire. At the same time, Travers considers what career path she might follow given her newfound love of the written word. She ponders the idea of becoming a journalist, but a friend warns her against the thought. He says that journalism is a dead end and stifles all creative energies. This was probably good advice, delivered at just the right time.

Throughout 1923, Travers applies herself to writing and achieves moderate success, in spite of the protests of Aunt Ellie. She submits erotic and sentimental poetry to *The Bulletin*. Among these pieces is "Keening," a fantasy poem that echoes her father's love of Irish folk tales and myths. For the most part, Travers's poetry is concerned with the body, youth, sensation, the physical world and the stars. Several of the recurring "characters" in her poetry are early versions of characters who will appear later in her fiction.

While *The Bulletin* proves to be a reliable outlet for her creative energy, it's *The Triad* literary magazine that gives Travers her big break. The magazine is run on a meager budget, and the editors often writer under false names to give the impression of a large crew of freelance reporters and writers. Frank Morton, one of the business partners on the magazine, replaces Allan Wilkie in the role of mentor to Travers. Aunt Ellie is again horrified at the idea of young Travers spending her time with "writers." She wonders if her spirited niece will ever settle into a definite groove, or simply keep hopping from one passion to the next.

Morton and his editing partner Charles Baeyertz invited Travers to join the staff of *The Triad* in May 1923. At the time, it was a trend among periodical magazines to devote some of their pages to female contributors. For the magazines, this was purely a smart business decision. Women of the time were demanding a greater voice in society. In addition, female readership of magazines was on a steady climb. Baeyertz and Morton knew they had struck gold when they hired Travers. They were so sure of her success that they gave her dominion over an entire section of the magazine. Entitled "A Woman Hits Back," Travers' contributions included her usual erotic poetry, fantasy literature and satire. The new section is a hit among readers.

Despite her position as a voice for women, Travers was not enthusiastic about feminism in general. She worried that her gender was trying to gain all the advantages of masculinity with none of the drawbacks, which would be impossible. She also becomes more and more unhappy with being in Australia. Travers believes the people are stuffy, rigid and lacking in a sense of humor. She, therefore, begins saving money for passage to England – more specifically Ireland – possibly chasing the dreams of her late father. As usual, Aunt Ellie is strongly opposed to the idea, but ultimately lends her support. In fact, she pays the fare for her young niece.

On February 9, 1924, Pamela Travers boards the *Medic* of Dalgety and Company for a 50-day voyage to Southampton. It was the beginning of a new chapter in her already adventurous life.

*   *   *   *   *

Despite almost crippling seasickness, Travers makes the most of her journey on board the *Medic*. On the way to England, the ship makes stops in both South Africa and the Canary Islands. On shore at these ports of call, Travers seeks out pertinent contacts in the newspaper and magazine industry. She looks up old friends of Allan Wilkie in the hopes of smoothing her transition into the wider world. In the meantime, she produces vibrant travel literature for the *Sun* and *The Triad*. Even half a world away, *The Triad* is still among the most faithful clients for her freelance writing.

Arriving in London after nearly two months at sea, Travers is greeted by well-to-do relatives – nieces and nephews of Aunt Ellie, in fact. She would later tell interviewers that she disembarked in London with only £20 to her name, £10 of which she immediately lost. These wealthy relatives don't share her enthusiasm for literature and the arts, encouraging Travers to join them for a holiday in Cannes. Instead, she remains in London, checking out the sights and sounds and knocking on the door of every editor's office in Bloomsbury. Her freelance earnings enable her to find an apartment close to Fleet Street, the publishing epicenter of London. Most of her earnings still come from the Christchurch *Sun*, which eagerly publishes everything she sends their way. Her marketability in New Zealand and Australia is even greater now that she's a transplant in the Mother Country.

Travers finds England to be a different place than she had anticipated. The land of her father's imagination was long gone. The mythical, fairy tale world was supplanted by the Great War, and a new breed of thinkers and writers were dominating the Empire's consciousness. William Butler Yeats was replaced by James Joyce, Virginia Wolfe and T. S. Eliot. Travers was a cultural outsider for the first time in her life, but her ambition was not squashed. At 1925's British Empire Exhibition, she sees King George V (from a distance) and immediately produces an account for her Australia and New Zealand readership.

In these early days, in England, Travers has already set her sights on publication in the half-political, half-literary periodical the *Irish Statesman*. The publisher is George William Russell, an intellectual giant with powerful connections on both sides of the Atlantic Ocean. She submits a few poems to Russell with no cover letter and holds her breath. To her amazement, the editor responds with praise, telling her that he will be more than happy to publish her work. He even asks that she come to visit him at his offices in Plunkett House, Dublin.

At one of their first meetings, Russell, who preferred the mystical initials AE, promises to publish more or less everything that Travers produces. She is introduced to an intimate circle of writers and thinkers. They include James Stephens, Padraic Colum, Oliver St. John Gogarty and Sean O'Faolain. Most impressive of all, however, is the revered William Butler Yeats. He is a God-like figure in Travers's eyes, and his positive endorsement of her creativity means everything. AE, for his part, becomes probably the most important mentor in Travers's line of mentors and kindred spirits. His fascination with the occult, the spirit world and reincarnation have a profound influence on Travers. The pair never become more than friends, but there is undoubtedly a magnetic attraction between the two from the very start. If AE had been younger, or maybe just bolder, something more romantic might have happened between them.

Despite new friends and plenty to keep her occupied, Travers never loses touch with family back in Australia. In 1925, she begins squirreling away extra money to pay for her mother's passage to England. She does this by writing for "ordinary" magazines, the 1920s equivalent of today's grocery store celebrity gossip pages. Naturally, she writes under an assumed name that bears no resemblance to her other pen names. Travers has a knack for the style and makes more than enough to bring her mother to visit and pay the rent and bills.

The primary themes in Travers's writing gradually undergo a change as she matures into a confident, cosmopolitan woman. The fixations with the body and eroticism remain, but new ideas emerge under the influence of AE, Yeats and their circle of Dublin artists and intellectuals. The idea of the public self as a mask worn to hide the true self is undeniably in the tradition of Yeats. Likewise, children, youth, imagination, fantasy and dreams become more prominent in her poetry and prose. Later, after the success of *Mary Poppins*, Travers would tell biographers and reviewers that she never considered herself a children's writer. Instead, she merely happened to write "about" children at certain points of her career.

By 1928, Travers had a roommate to ease the burden of rent. She and Madge Burnand, daughter of a moderately famous playwright, became fast friends and lived together for ten years. They went on European holidays together, traveling to Spain, Italy and points between. Biographers are not sure how close their relationship was. At the same time, Travers was continuing to diversify her writing. She was moving away from the simplistic journalism required by *The Triad* or the *Sun* and towards more complex, nuanced prose.

The tragic and unexpected death of Travers's mother in November 1928 partially contributes to a worsening of her own health. She suffers from bouts of pleurisy and fatigue. She again experiences her morbid dread of tuberculosis, a neurotic frame of mind that persists her whole life. Her letters to AE often dwell on her sense of being ill. How much of this illness was real and how much was hypochondria is unknown. At any rate, doctors advise her to live outside the crowded confines of London while her body recuperates. In the summer of 1931, she begins thinking about a mythical or fantasy story while resting in a sanitarium. However, she is too concerned with her physical wellbeing to follow her creative impulse beyond the formation of an idea.

Leaving the sanitarium, Travers and Burnand move into a rustic cottage in Mayfield, far off the beaten path. In 1932, feeling remarkably better than she had in years, Travers takes a trip to Soviet Russia. Her travel articles from the journey are compiled into her first full-length book: *Moscow Excursion*. Published in 1934, AE praised *Moscow Excursion* for its sense of humor and keen eye for detail. Travers disguised her authorship as "P. T." The book was dedicated to "HLG," perhaps meaning herself, Helen Lyndon Goff.

The friendship between Travers and AE was ten year's strong when AE's health began to decline. He lost his love for Ireland, and the comrades of his own generation were slowly slipping away. He was no longer the powerful mentor figure he once was. Still, he was able to offer some important assistance to Travers even near the end. AE introduced his young protégée to the publisher Alfred Richard Orage. The *Irish Statesman* and *The New Triad* had effectively ran their course as journalistic projects, and Travers was in search of new ground to plow. As publisher of the *New English Weekly*, Orage offered Travers the chance to continue publishing her poetry, but by 1933, she had given up the role of "poetess." Instead, she became the magazine's drama critic.

Chapter Four: Mary Poppins

The Mary Poppins series consisted of eight books published between 1934 and 1988. The title character is a mysterious but professional nanny who has a knack for setting things right. In the universe of the books, time has no meaning and no effect. The Banks children and the neighborhood of Cherry Tree Lane never change. Mary Poppins appears and disappears like an inexplicable force of nature. Travers never could explain where her most famous character came from or where she went at the end of each novel. She simply existed, and that was enough. In discussions with critics and interviewers, Travers reveals relatively little about the origins of her most famous literary character. Academics have explored the mythical underpinnings of the Poppins character, demonstrating that the stories do indeed go well beyond just children's literature. Still, it's possible to make meaningful connections between the world of Mary Poppins and the life times of her author, P. L. Travers.

Origins of Mary Poppins

Travers has been recorded as saying that Mary Poppins always existed inside of her. The character was just waiting for the opportunity to reveal herself to the author. Briefly, Mary Poppins is a combination of Travers's childhood memories, daydreams, family, mysticism, poetry and even a moderate kind of feminism. One might say that Travers *is* Poppins, but the opposite is not necessarily true: Poppins is much more than one person. She is a collection of personalities, ideas, values and beliefs that capture both the creative mind of the author and the time and place of her imaginative creation.

To understand Mary Poppins is to learn more about Travers than she was normally comfortable revealing to outsiders. She had a personal theory on womanhood that she only rarely expressed. She believed that all women passed through three phases in their life: Maiden, Mother and Crone. The characters in the Poppins books display these phases in various degrees. Poppins, at one time or another, displays all three. She is a Maiden because she is young and still has a spark in her life. She's a bit unpredictable. Poppins is also a Mother, taking excellent care of her charges. And last but not least, she is a Crone, full of the wisdom of the ancients. Travers explains that, while, in one sense, Poppins is in her twenties, in another she's timeless and ageless. The other magical characters in the books, many of them ancient, always greet Travers as a familiar personage.

The setting of the Mary Poppins novels is Cherry Tree Lane, a mythical side street in a suburban neighborhood of London. In interviews, Travers has said that the neighborhood was meant to resemble Chelsea around 1900 or 1910. However, it's nothing like the bustling, modern city that Travers inhabited in 1924. Instead, it's more like the mythical, exotic, fairy tale London that fired Travers's imagination as a child and young adult. It's Edwardian London, with a sense of rules, order and optimism that had faded by the time the Modern Age dawned. It's the London that she hoped to find when she boarded the *Medic* in 1924, fueled with youthful optimism. Travers imagined a world before the blight of the Great War changed humanity's sense of place and history. The stability and predictability of Cherry Tree Lane are things that Travers rarely if ever enjoyed in her own tumultuous life.

People from Travers's youth are frequently the inspiration for characters in the Mary Poppins books. As a child in Bowral, for instance, she met several unforgettable characters who would live again in the pages of fiction, such as Nellie Rubina and Uncle Dodger (*Mary Poppins Comes Back*). But by far the most influential inspiration for the Mary Poppins character was Aunt Ellie. As a powerful matriarch, Aunt Ellie seemed to wield unquestionable power and influence. She was the stabilizing force in young Travers's life, the one who stepped in and set things right that had gone wrong. She was also a woman full of contradictions. At any moment, she could be harsh or loving, humble or proud, but regardless of her moods, she always had Travers's best interests at heart. Aunt Ellie came from another time and place, a generation removed from her niece's world. Conservative tendencies dominated her taste and decisions.

Literary influences are also profoundly important in the development of the world of *Mary Poppins*. The two most obvious predecessors to Travers's novels are *Alice in Wonderland* and *Peter Pan*. She had a high regard for *Alice in Wonderland*, enjoying the way that Lewis Carroll mixed fantastic elements with the ordinary. Travers was particularly fond of J. M. Barrie, the playwright behind *Peter Pan*. She may even have borrowed the style of initialing her pen name (P. L.) from Barrie. The elements of *Peter Pan* that she most enjoyed were the wonder of flying, the timeless nature of the nursery, and the realization of adult concepts like mortality and fear.

Writing and Publication

Much of the actual writing of the first Mary Poppins novel took place at Pound Cottage, the rustic, rural retreat near Mayfield that Travers shared with Madge Burnand. Sorting through old scrapbooks and journals, Travers noticed the recurring "Poppins" character, along with other characters sharing similar magical qualities. She had shown these stories to friends, including AE, who suggested that she expand on the work and create a full-length novel. AE saw in the character an opportunity to present the world with a mythical, legendary that exemplified many of his beliefs about the nature of consciousness and the universe. Travers was not so ambitious. Instead, she intended to reveal how the "ordinary" world and the world of magical imagination were the same.

With her health always in question, Travers had periods of low energy, but still finished the first Poppins novel in a short period. The urging of friends AE provided her with needed motivation. She showed the completed manuscript to Burnand, who was immediately convinced of its greatness.

As the daughter of a well-connected publisher, Burnand was instrumental in helping Travers bring her book to market. She took the finished manuscript to London and shopped it to a slew of editor friends. Gerald Howe, manager of a small publishing operation, expressed his interest in meeting the author. According to Travers, the pair got off on the wrong foot. In fact, she never let go of the thought that he was an "enemy" working against her best interests. Travers found a publication partner in America through the publishing house of Eugene Reynal.

Mary Poppins (1934)

The first Mary Poppins book introduces all of the key characters who will re-appear in the subsequent books. The Banks house at 17 Cherry Tree Lane is the most dilapidated on the block, its outer appearance mirroring the family dysfunction on the inside. The book is divided into twelve chapters. In chapter one, Poppins arrives floating on the east wind. In the last chapter, she departs on the west wind, parrot-headed umbrella in hand. The intervening chapters each contain a magical, self-contained adventure. In a sense, they almost function as independent short stories.

In the original publication of *Mary Poppins*, the chapter entitled "Bad Tuesday" featured a whirlwind trip across the globe, and a visit to both north and south poles. The story also included some not-so-politically correct stereotypes of people of different ethnicities, such as the Inuit people, Chinese and Native Americans. In the 1960s, a teacher friend of Travers's described how awkward it was to read the chapter to young children of color. Travers happily rewrote the chapter, altering certain words and phrases, but leaving the essence intact. However, by the early 1980s, even these revisions were not enough. Travers again rewrote the chapter. This time, the children visited animal representatives rather than people. Harcourt initially printed 5,000 copies of the "revised edition."

Mary Poppins Comes Back (1935)

The follow-up to *Mary Poppins* arrives only one year after the original. Thematically and structurally, it's a mirror image of the first book. Chapter titles have been cleverly altered, and the adventures are different, but essentially *Mary Poppins Comes Back* is a continuation story. The Banks family is still having difficulties. One day, Michael flies a kite in the park and finds Poppins on the other end when he reels in the string. The children visit a magical circus in space, have a bizarre tea party, and meet Miss Andrew. When Poppins leaves, she has a return ticket in her hand, leaving the door open for another adventure.

Mary Poppins Opens the Door (1943)

The third Mary Poppins book took shape during World War II, while Travers and Camillus were evacuees in America. Her American publisher urged her to work on a new book of adventures for the now world-famous Edwardian nanny. At first, Travers considered titling the book *Good-bye Mary Poppins*, thinking it would be the last one. Her publisher was horrified. The series was marketable and profitable, a golden goose that he didn't want to see leave the coop. He suggested an alternate, suitably vague title: *Mary Poppins Opens the Door*.

Not departing from the successful formula of the first two Poppins book, *Mary Poppins Opens the Door* sees the children go on a series of adventures. They always return home with newfound insight or perspective.

Mary Poppins in the Park (1952)

The American publisher, Eugene Reynal, once again leaned on the now 53-year-old Travers for another Poppins book. In the beginning, she had agreed to produce four such books for the publisher. He began to feel that the fourth was overdue. With some reluctance, she sat down to compose what she once more believed was her last series of adventures with Mary Poppins. *Mary Poppins in the Park* features six adventures that took place within the chronology of the second or third Poppins book. The idea of the park is a framing device for the individual stories. Each one begins and ends in the park, a place that's given mystical significance by Travers.

Mary Poppins From A to Z (1962)

Mary Poppins from A to Z is a departure from the previous Mary Poppins books. Each page represented a letter of the alphabet and was accompanied by an illustration from Mary Shepard. However, Shepard by this time knew of Travers's movie deal with Disney. She felt left out and betrayed. Fairly or not, she felt entitled to some portion of the windfall that her creative partner was going to receive. She pushed back against Travers, asking for a higher wage, and threatening some kind of legal action if any of her images were associated with the film. *Mary Poppins from A to Z* was translated into Latin during her residence at Smith College.

Mary Poppins in the Kitchen (1975)

This entry to the series is exactly what it sounds like. The Banks family cook has left, and Poppins steps in to pick up the burden. All of the "adventures" happen in the kitchen. At the back of the book are numerous recipes.

Mary Poppins in Cherry Tree Lane (1982)

In a return to form, *Mary Poppins in Cherry Tree Lane* again features the ageless nanny taking the Banks children on strange, wonderful adventures. The events of the book take place on midsummer's eve, supposedly a magical time in the Poppins universe.

Mary Poppins and the House Next Door (1988)

The last Mary Poppins is the most shadowy and mysterious of all. It concerns the appearance of a boy from the South Seas, Luti. He is friendly to everyone, but he needs help returning to his homeland. Meanwhile, the "house next door" – 18 Cherry Tree Lane, to be exact – presents a mystery to the Banks family. Mr. Banks imagines that an old astronomer lives there, gazing toward the stars as he seeks to understand the universe.

Reaction to the Novels

Mary Poppins enjoyed success far beyond Travers's expectations, but this didn't necessarily equal fame and fortune. Her choice of a vague pen name – P. L. Travers – ensured her a certain degree of anonymity. She said that she didn't want the author of *Mary Poppins* to be identifiable as a man or women. Instead, she wanted Poppins herself to be the focal point of the novel. This desire for anonymity would be a recurring theme, as well as an internal contradiction, throughout Travers's life.

By 1982, the American publisher Harcourt Brace Jovanivoch had sold more than 1.5 million hardcover editions of the Mary Poppins books. However, the company resisted the idea of releasing a paperback, mass-market edition. Delacorte/Dell offered to buy the paperback rights for $100,000, but Harcourt refused. Eventually, Delacorte did secure the rights, and the book has continued to be in print since its initial release.

Reviewers generally heaped praise on all of the Poppins novels, to varying degrees. However, the perception that they were merely "children's literature" was something that irked Travers for the rest of her life. She even made snappish comments to interviewers, such as, "I don't write for children – I turn my back on them." This, among other things, helped create a public perception that Travers was kind of a snob.

Chapter Five: Mary Poppins Film (1964)

Even from the initial publication of *Mary Poppins*,
film and TV executives, including the legendary
mogul Walt Disney, had expressed interest in buying
the rights to the stories. For nearly twenty years,
Travers was adamantly opposed to the idea. However,
she understood that, from the book-buying public's
point of view, Mary Poppins was her only memorable
achievement. This was a depressing realization, but
motivated her to keep producing Poppins novels –
even though she guaranteed that each one was the
last. Disney was unrelenting in his efforts to acquire
the movie rights. Endlessly patient and persistent, he
expected to succeed in the end, and he did.

In 1959, life events conspired to change Travers's thoughts about a Mary Poppins movie. Her estranged friend Madge Burnand died in a hospital after a lengthy illness. The two had suffered a falling out before the Second World War. Attempts at reconciliation nearly always ended in raised voices or even violence. Travers found new female companions to take Burnand's place, including the painter Gertrude Hermes and the publisher's daughter Jessie Orage. Still, she took Burnand's death hard, possibly angry with herself that they never mended their relationship. At the same time, her adopted son Camillus was going through profound personal issues. He had discovered, entirely by accident, that he was adopted and not Travers's biological son. This began a downward spiral of heavy drinking and other destructive behaviors. Camillus had his driver's license revoked. Then, pulled over by the police for drunk driving without a license, he was sentenced to six months in prison. Travers was at her wit's end.

The four Mary Poppins books were always in print and had achieved fair, but not overwhelming success. There was certainly a "cult" of devoted fans, including Disney's young daughter Diane, but the books by no means made Travers a rich woman. Royalties had been modest, but were beginning to taper off. Travers's income from freelance writing and a weekly lodger were barely enough to pay the bills. With friends passing away, an adopted son in legal trouble and a financial wall staring her in the face, Travers decided it was time to relent. She notified her lawyers that she was open to the possibility of an arrangement with the Walt Disney organization. But, she told them, the conditions of her agreement would be strict and non-negotiable.

In July 1959, Travers received a letter from her New York lawyer, Arnold Goodman, concerning the terms for the sale of movie rights for Mary Poppins to Walt Disney. Goodman and Disney's representatives – William Dover and Mr. Swan – had for several months been carefully negotiating a deal for the rights. The result was a lucrative arrangement for Travers, but required her to give up substantial control to the studio. The title of the film would be *Walt Disney's Mary Poppins*, clearly indicating who was in charge of the medium and the message. Travers would receive a $100,000 down payment once the film treatment had passed muster. Upon release of the film, she would receive 5% of the producer's gross – revenue after accounting for the costs of production and distribution. The deal was simply too sweet for Travers to pass up, especially given her financial situation.

The terms of the deal stated that Travers would be involved in production and filming as a "consultant." In reality, she would not have much input into the eventual film. Disney and his writing team had a set idea of who Mary Poppins was, and she was unrecognizable from the character in the books. They imagined a character that was all sweetness and light, with a beautiful singing voice and angelic face. The movie would have no darkness or sadness and certainly no ambiguity. Grudgingly, Travers accepted this state of affairs but only up to a point. She realized that film was a different medium and that Walt Disney wanted to tell a particular kind of story to a particular audience. However, she still pushed back on several key decisions. For one, she strongly resisted the idea of a romance between Mary and Bert. She was also determined to see the film's setting be true to the book: Edwardian England, and not an animated wonderland. Some of the writers had considered modernizing the setting, but thankfully, this was abandoned. Lastly, she was determined that the cast be entirely British. An Americanized, accent-free Poppins was a horrifying idea to her.

Travers's first "job" as consultant was to come up with a treatment for the film – essentially a rough draft of the action and story arc. She was given 60 days, but found the work to be slow and tedious. Having never written for television before, she hired the accomplished TV scriptwriter Donald Bull to work alongside her. The resulting treatment was too bloated for a film, and was nothing like what the Disney people had in mind. She hoped to include 17 distinct "adventures" from her four Mary Poppins books. At the same time, she wanted to maintain the air of mystery and symbolism that was so important to her work. The treatment was submitted on time, after which Travers could only wait. As days turned into weeks, Travers worried that Disney was abandoning the project. A few nervous messages later, and she was assured that everything was on course.

Between December 1959 and February 1960, veteran Disney writer Bill Walsh, among others, carved and sliced at Travers's treatment, turning her ambiguous, artsy Poppins into a warm, sentimental, smiling angel from the clouds. The eventual script was much leaner, with only a handful of original Poppins adventures. The essential frame of the story, however, was preserved. Mary Poppins arrived on the east wind and departed on the west wind. During her stay with the Bankses, she solved problems, taught essential life lessons, and generally brought the family closer together.

Travers had the benefit of sitting in on the storyboarding and scripting process, a nerve-wracking several days of objections and frustrations. She was horrified by some of the ideas being floated by the writers. She was primarily concerned that the team didn't "get" the books or Mary Poppins. The writers deferred to her as consultant on several points, but secretly they were annoyed by her constant objections. She won the day on a few points, but mostly the writers stuck to their guns. As far as casting was concerned, Travers was primarily adamant that English actors be used in all the principal parts of the film. On this issue, as well as the Edwardian setting, she had her way.

The production of *Walt Disney's Mary Poppins* brought two powerful but diametrically opposed personalities into each other's orbits. Travers's and Disney's profound differences can be summed up quite simply: He was an entertainer, and she was an artist. He had a purely American vision of the happy, nuclear family, with conflicts peacefully resolved and everything in its right place. He wasn't interested in artistry, subtlety, symbolism or "difficult" fiction.

Travers was home in London throughout the filming. The only contact she had with the film studio was through Julie Andrews, a casting choice of which she greatly approved. Ultimately, however, there were countless elements in the movie that offended her sensibilities. Travers especially disliked the musical number, "It's a Jolly Holiday with Mary." The scene, during which Mary, the Banks children and Bert leap into a sidewalk chalk drawing and have magical adventures, was borrowed from Travers's 1926 story "Mary Poppins and the Match Man." Travers disliked seeing her characters interact with cartoon animals. She found it all too over the top and ridiculous.

The premier of *Walt Disney's Mary Poppins* was set for August 27, 1964 at Grauman's Chinese Theatre. Travers waited impatiently for an invitation to the showing. She pestered her lawyer for news, and then finally a personal note arrived asking her to attend. Her American publisher was ready to set her up in a Hollywood hotel while Disney was paying the airfare. The event was pure spectacle. Disney characters lined the sidewalks while the media gravitated to Walt. Travers felt lost in the shuffle. Many guests had no idea who she was. As the movie began, she cried at the enormity of seeing her Edwardian nanny come to life on the screen.

Walt Disney's Mary Poppins was an enormous hit in the United States. Nearly every leading critic heaped praise on the film. The movie cost approximately $5 million to make, but eventually grossed more the $75 million. It launched the career of Julie Andrews and made Dick Van Dyke a household name. *Mary Poppins* was also one of the first films to unleash the marketing juggernaut for which Disney is now so famous. Cloths, dolls, jewelry and books were all produced to tie in with the film. Disney even released "adapted" Mary Poppins children's books, which far outsold Travers's source material, despite receiving a healthy bump from the film.

Hints and rumors of a possible sequel persisted for some time following the release of *Walt Disney's Mary Poppins*. However, Disney himself had never produced a sequel and claimed that he was opposed to them. For purely financial reasons, and partly out of fear of Disney, Travers promoted the idea of a second Poppins film. She even said that she would speak with Julie Andrews and convince her to reprise her role. All thoughts of a second film were quashed in 1966. Disney reported to his company that there were no plans for a sequel. He died of lung cancer later that year.

As the initial glow of the film faded, and Travers felt more secure expressing her true feelings, she began to reveal how she actually responded to Disney's adaptation. She told interviewers in England that the film was all wrong and that Walt Disney had tricked her, cheapening the value of her work. For the remainder of her life, she carried a quiet grudge against Disney for stealing her glory. Still, this grudge did not stop her from entertaining further offers of movies and stage productions down the road.

By January 1988, the Disney film studio was again considering the idea of a *Mary Poppins* sequel. Once more, Travers's involvement and agreement would be important. The film would mirror the novel *Mary Poppins Comes Back*. Once more, the terms of the deal were attractive, but by this time, Travers hardly needed the money. Disney offered her an advance of $100,000 for the rights, $25,000 for the writing of a treatment, and 2.5 percent of gross profits. BBC radio star Brian Sibley was tasked with helping draft the treatment. The plot involved the imminent failure of Mr. Banks's bank, a resonant theme given the worldwide financial problems of the 1980s. Readers of the treatment were positive and encouraging. Ultimately, the plan fell through. Disney believed the project would be too expensive and, therefore, too risky.

Chapter Six: Later Career

P. L. Travers was entering her 65th year when *Walt Disney's Mary Poppins* hit the big screen. Her life was transitioning from one of restless activity to one of somber, quiet reflection. She was becoming the wise old women, the "crone" of her feminine myth structure. At times, she pushed back against this reality. Certain disappointments in her life – her adopted son, her failed romances – nagged at her. Disney's film seemed to cheapen her most noteworthy accomplishment. Still, Travers forged ahead, trusting that more growth, discovery and enlightenment were in her future.

In the autumn of 1965, Barbara Solomon, one of the deans of Radcliffe College, invited Travers to live on campus as a "writer in residence." The idea of a writer in residence was a new one in the mid-60s. No one, least of all Travers, was sure what such a person would do with his or her time. College staff converted some rooms into a suite for the visiting dignitary in Whitman Hall, part of Radcliffe's East House. Prior to arrival, she gave strict instructions as to how she was to be received. For example, she didn't want to be mobbed by reporters the moment she arrived. Essentially, Travers needed everything about her stay to be on her terms. She hoped that the student body would flock to her and glean from her the wisdom she had to offer. The reality of her semester at Radcliffe, unfortunately, fell short of her ideals.

Travers spends much of her time in the Widener Library, studying mythology and fairy tales. She found she liked the modest college library much better than the stuffy British Museum library. At Radcliffe, she begins work on her first purely academic work, an investigation of the origins of the Sleeping Beauty myth. She also gives occasional interviews to college newspapers and local radio stations. Professors and students alike have mixed reactions to Travers. While to some she is matronly and warm, to others she seems harsh and unapproachable.

In early 1966, she leaves Radcliffe. However, the experience was so enjoyable that she sends letters to a few more colleges to inquire about writer in residence opportunities. Smith College, also located in Massachusetts, responds in the affirmative. Travers once again settles into a quaint suite on a college campus for the fall semester, 1966. Like Radcliffe, Smith College is an all-girls school. The students cover all the bases of a liberal education, but many of them will do nothing further in the world than get married and have children. Things have changed in the United States by 1966, though, especially among younger people. Opposition to the Vietnam War has grown to dull roar, and the college generation is poised to shake up the status quo. The Summer of Love is only a few years away. For her part, Travers is uninterested in these social upheavals. She has grown into a stodgy conservative. The chasm between her and the students she is supposed to be mentoring has become too wide to cross.

Although she didn't realize it, Travers's fame was quickly fading. She urges several faculty members at Smith College to help her bring about Latin and Russian translations of *Mary Poppins*. They humor her, but progress is slow. Many of the professors find her to be pretentious and out of touch. Travers is both self-conscious and secretive as a writer in residence. She is defensive about the fact that she never attended college herself. Likewise, she provides inaccurate birth dates for herself, hesitates to name Australia as her homeland, and provides fanciful but not actually real stories from her childhood. Despite her steady slide into obscurity, Travers is determined to be the author of her own story.

Despite her advancing age and lifelong struggle with what today might be diagnosed as irritable bowel syndrome, Travers stayed almost obsessively busy throughout the late 1960s and 1970s. In 1968, she released the *Mary Poppins Story for Coloring*, perhaps trying to milk the last remnants of her association with Disney. Of course, the royalty checks would always be more than enough to sustain her, but she told many friends that she felt poor even in her wealth. She was looking for a spiritual sustenance. She went from one guru or doctor to another, searching for healing and wholeness.

Travers's tried and failed to get "outside" of the Mary Poppins box that she found herself in. From 1966 to 1971, she worked falteringly on a new story entitled *Friend Monkey*. The story concerned a poor family and a monkey from India that was, in fact, the physical manifestation of a Hindu god. This god meant well for everyone but more frequently caused chaos. The story reads like an anti-Mary Poppins, and so isn't much of a departure from the Poppins themes at all. Halfway through the writing process, the manuscript is lost, forcing Travers to start over. When it's finally published in 1971, critics pan the book and readers ignore it. Unsold volumes are shipped back to the publishing house. Travers is bitterly disappointed, not comprehending how people can dismiss what she believes to be her best work.

In the spring of 1970, Travers once more tries to find solitude and an atmosphere conducive to work as writer in residence at California's Scripps College. She is also awarded the Clark lectureship at Scripps. Her lecture topic concerns the enduring power of myth and fairy tales. Travers's stay at the college was not memorable, since she barely interacted with the student body. Instead, she spends much of her time putting the finishing touches on *Friend Monkey*.

After her awkward semester at Scripps College and more unsuccessful attempts to improve her health, Travers settles into an apartment in Manhattan. Ever since her first visit, she maintained a kind of spiritual connection with New York City. There, she entertains New Age-minded guests, distilling the lessons she's learned from countless gurus. At the same time, she fights to keep her name in the public imagination. In 1972, she donates a collection of Mary Poppins-related trinkets to the New York Public Library. At the donation ceremony, Travers is proud and aloof. Few approach her or dare to ask questions. A *New York Times* headline reads "Mary Poppins as a Zen Monk."

Travers had been working steadily on her Sleeping Beauty project ever since the fall of 1965 at Radcliffe. In 1975, McGraw-Hill publishes *About the Sleeping Beauty*. The series of five retellings of the Sleeping Beauty myth attempt to reach the core or essence of world mythology. Most readers ignore the book. Academics in America complain that the book is self-absorbed and preachy. British reviewers are kinder, but nevertheless the book is seen as a failure.

At this point, Travers owned two homes in England, and she was renting an apartment in New York. The tax burden of living stateside was becoming a drain on her resources. It wasn't practical anymore, and she longed to return to England. She moved back to her London home and worked occasionally on a collection of her letters and essays. Soon after her return home, an old friend from America, Dorothea Darling, reached out to Travers with a proposition. Darling was in the process of launching a semi-academic journal relating to mythology, tradition and New Age thinking called *Parabola*. She wondered if Travers might like to be founding editor or contributor, or both. Travers quickly agreed, contributing to most issues while she was alive.

In 1977, the first of two great honors is bestowed upon Travers. The Queen announces that Travers has been granted the Order of the British Empire. The following year, Pittsburgh's Chatham College awards the author with an honorary doctorate in humane letters. From then on, Travers insists that she be called "doctor" rather than miss. The honorary degree feels like a vindication of her academic hopes and dreams.

In her personal life, Travers continues to search desperately for meaning and answers. She becomes a sort of guru herself, with younger people coming to hear her speak. However, few people ask her questions. As always, her demeanor is intimidating and proud. In her quiet time, she begins to think seriously of another Mary Poppins book. She also thinks seriously of her own mortality, wondering which might happen first – a new book or the end of life.

Travers continued working to compile all of her literary papers, essays and personal letters, almost to the point of obsession. A fear of going broke occupied her mind, despite her millions in the bank. Her agent shopped the collection to numerous American universities, but the market for literary collections was not at a high point. Therefore, the price tag was set at $75,000 Australian dollars. At the same time, Travers begins drafting a new Mary Poppins adventure. She writes much of the new book while spending the summer months in Switzerland. *Mary Poppins in Cherry Tree Lane* was released in 1982. The book receives positive reviews, and Travers feels that it's the best of the series.

In her constant quest to stay productive and engaged with the world, Travers attempts to bring Mary Poppins back to life in new media, specifically the stage. She strikes up a creative partnership with Broadway producer Jules Fisher in 1981. Fisher agrees to help her bring Poppins to the theater. The pair agree that a musical would be the most appropriate genre. Fisher suggests several possible writers, including Tim Rice and Tom Stoppard. He truly wanted the expertise of Steven Sondheim, but he was too absorbed in other projects. Travers objected to Sondheim because he was too modern and edgy. She floated the somewhat absurd idea of having former Beatle Paul McCartney write the lyrics.

The search for a writer proves fruitless, and Fisher and Travers find themselves back at the drawing board on more than one occasion. Fisher discovers that the author is extremely demanding and exacting. He doubts that any production would satisfy her requirements. By 1988, they part ways, having accomplished nothing other than the spending of more than $200,000. Travers tells Fisher that she'll simply write the stage treatment herself. He advises her that while she is certainly a talented writer, stage writing is a far different project.

Early in 1984, Disney contacted Travers to gauge her interest in a possible television series. Representing the TV studio, Ed Self visits her Shawfield Street home to discuss particulars. An initial six episodes would be produced as a test, with $86,000 in consultant fees paid to Travers. Enthusiasm for the project is high on all sides, but details are few and far between. Like so many of her late-life plans, the TV series never materializes.

In 1988, Travers published her last Mary Poppins book, *Mary Poppins and the House Next Door*. In one sense, the book is a farewell and homecoming for Travers. Poppins herself is not the focus of the book. Instead, the story follows a mysterious visitor from the South Seas. His return home is a kind of spiritual return home for Travers who, apart from a single visit in the 1960s, never once returned to Australia. Her agents and publishers praise the book, and the reviews are generally warm.

Travers's collection of personal papers languished for most of the 1980s. Finally, in 1989, the Mitchell Library in Sydney agreed to purchase them for $20,000. Travers is bitterly disappointed, but resigned to the fact that she has become truly unknown once more.

Travers's last book is published in 1989. *What the Bee Knows* is a collection of essays originally written for *Parabola*. As such, the work is dense and almost incomprehensible for those not familiar with New Age philosophies – a self-contained book doesn't attract much attention. The last few years of Travers's life are spent almost entirely in seclusion. She has nurses to care for her, and she receives occasional visits from Camillus, her grandchildren, or old friends and colleagues. In 1995, a few reporters visit to inquire about another possible staging of *Mary Poppins*, but once more the idea never blossoms into reality. Travers dies quietly in the spring of 1996 with her son by her side.

Conclusion: Legacy

Thanks to the Mary Poppins series of books, Travers's legacy will no doubt be enduring. Her contributions to both children's literature and to New Age philosophies were profound. In her personal life, she frequently battled with loneliness, physical illness, and a sense of being misunderstood. Her creative productions carry a hint of that suffering and pain. As a character, Mary Poppins has entered the popular culture, now delighting several generations of readers. Her witty and pointed sayings are part of the cultural vocabulary. The Walt Disney film production remains one of the most recognizable adaptations of children's literature ever made.

Today, Mary Poppins continues to be a powerful, almost unavoidable influence on anyone writing for children or young adults. *Harry Potter* author J. K. Rowling is a devoted fan, even borrowing Travers's style of writing her name. Travers always claimed that she didn't writer for children, and that may be true, but in writing for adults, she spoke to something childlike in everyone. Her work bridges a gap between fantasy and reality, showing how they are, in fact, not the separate entities we believe. Instead, fantasy and imagination are integral parts of reality.

Bibliography

Demers, Patricia. *P. L. Travers*. Boston: G. K. Hall & Co, 1991.

Lawson, Valerie. *Mary Poppins, She Wrote*. New York: Simon & Schuster, 1999.

"P. L. Travers." (2013). Encyclopedia of World Biography.
http://www.notablebiographies.com/supp/Supplement-Sp-Z/Travers-P-L.html

"P. L. Travers." (2013). Wikipedia.
http://en.wikipedia.org/wiki/P._L._Travers#Books_on_P._L._Travers

Picardie, Justin. (2008). "Was P L Travers the Real Mary Poppins?" *The Telegraph*, Oct. 28.

http://www.telegraph.co.uk/culture/donotmigrate/3562643/Was-P-L-Travers-the-real-Mary-Poppins.html

"Mary Poppins." (2013). Wikipedia.
http://en.wikipedia.org/wiki/Mary_poppins

"Mary Poppins (film)." (2013). Wikipedia.
http://en.wikipedia.org/wiki/Mary_Poppins_(film)

Made in the USA
Lexington, KY
31 December 2013